Japanese for English Speakers

R. Healing

Japanese Grammar for English Speakers

This book is an introduction to the Japanese language for native English speakers.

Having taught Japanese in England for many years, I have found the various textbooks I have used lacking in some respects. I hope to include in this book the answers to many of the questions asked by students but not necessarily, to my mind, answered sufficiently clearly till now.

I shall deal with one topic at a time, with the answers to the tests and questions printed at the end of the book.

If you go to Japan - and I really recommend that you do: it is a beautiful country and the people are delightful - and you manage to say even a few words of Japanese, you will be highly complimented on your proficiency which, of course, boosts your confidence and urges you on to more speaking.

I hope you enjoy the book and find it useful - apologies for my dreadful artistic ability!

All photos used in this book were taken by us during our visits to Japan

Rosemary Healing

Cheerful god at Beppu

INDEX

Introduction 2

Basic Japanese Grammar 6

The sound of the Japanese language 9

The written language 12

Chapter 1	Basic grammar	16
	Practice 1 (a)	17
	Practice 1 (b)	18
Chapter 2	Borrowed words	20
	Practice 2 (a)	20
	Practice 2 (b)	21
Chapter 3	Greetings and introductions	22
	Practice 3	24
Chapter 4	Nationality and language	25
	Practice 4	25
Chapter 5	Belonging	26
	Practice 5	26
Chapter 6	Numbers	27
	Practice 6 (a)	28
	Bigger numbers	29
	Practice 6 (b)	29
	Kanji numbers	30
	Counters	32
	Practice 6 (c)	34
Chapter 7	This and that, here and there	35
	Practice 7	37
Chapter 8	Question words	38
	Practice 8	39
Chapter 9	Post positional particles so far	41
	Practice 9	42
Chapter 10	Dates and days	43
	Practice 10	45
	Seasons	47
	Geography	48

Chapter 11	Verbs	49
	Practice 11	50
Chapter 12	Coming and going	51
	Practice 12 (a)	51
	Practice 12 (b)	52
Chapter 13	Existence and fact	53
	Practice 13	54
Chapter 14	Prepositions	55
	Practice 14	56
Chapter 15	Family	57
	(No practice 15)	
Chapter 16	Giving and receiving	58
	(No practice 16)	
Chapter 17	More particles	59
	Practice 17	59
	Also	60
	Nobody and nothing	60
Chapter 18	And	61
	Practice 18	61
Chapter 19	Taking leave	62
	Random revision exercises	65
	Answers	66
	Glossary - Japanese/English	75
	Glossary - English/Japanese	84
	Writing practice charts	94

Three wise monkeys, Nikko

Basic Japanese Grammar

To begin with, Japanese grammar is a great deal easier to master than other people's grammar. It does become more difficult later on ... The following notes may be useful:

There is no masculine or feminine in Japanese. That is to say you don't have to remember "la table" and "le livre".

A verb will take the same form whether it refers to one person or several.

There are three groups of verbs: all the verbs in Group I will decline in the same way, all the verbs in Group II will decline in their way and only the verbs in Group III will be slightly different - which is why they are in Group III - and there are only two of them.

There are hardly any singulars or plurals - in other words, the nouns themselves don't change but are modified by something which indicates whether there is only one or there are several. All will become clear later on.

One of the most important rules is that the main verb of the sentence always comes last. You might say in English, "This is the sweater that I bought yesterday at the supermarket for £5." In Japanese this could be, "This is yesterday at the supermarket for £5 sweater bought."

You will notice that in the above sentence "I" was omitted. Again we will deal with this later, but generally speaking pronouns are not used much in Japanese, and if it is you saying the sentence, it will be you who bought the sweater.

A small problem in Japanese is that there is quite a large number of homonyms: that is to say words that sound the same but mean different things. To give a couple of examples, *kin* can mean an old unit of weight, a muscle, bacteria or fungus and a prohibition. *Go* could mean the number 5, the Japanese board game, a word or language, afterwards or later on, a file or a line and an honorific prefix. Usually a word like this would be combined with another word so that the meaning would be clear, and in any case, often they would be distinguishable by being written differently.

Of course, we have many homonyms in English too, for example:

Pitch: The sound of a particular musical note

             The field on which cricket and other sports are played

             To throw something (a ball)

             The angle of a leaning roof (pitched)

             Black, sticky tar-like substance

             Putting up a tent etc.

You cannot express other people's thoughts in Japanese. You can't say, as you can in English, "He thinks he's a vampire." (*kyūketsuki* if you would like to know). In Japanese, you would have to say "It appears that he thinks he's a vampire", or "He tells me that he thinks he is a vampire".

There are three levels of speech in Japanese: honorific, polite and humble. These will be used according to the status of the speaker and listener. For example, the verb "to give", which we shall meet later on, would be *ageru* in the ordinary polite form, *sashiageru* if you are giving to someone of higher standing than yourself, and *kudasaru* if the superior person is giving to you.

In this book we shall only use the ordinary polite form.

Koshikawa Korakuen Gardens, Tokyo

The sound of the Japanese language

Japanese is a syllabic language: that is to say that, apart from the sound "*n*", every consonant has a vowel attached to it. Thus the Japanese "alphabet" is called a syllabary.

The basic vowel sounds are *a, i, u, e, o* in that order. They appear to be the same as in English, but are pronounced as follows:

Under the evening moon the cherry blossoms

a	i	u	e	o
a	i	u	e	o
ka	ki	ku	ke	ko
sa	shi	su	se	so
ta	chi	tsu	te	to
na	ni	nu	ne	no
ha	hi	fu	he	ho

The *ka* line hardened becomes *ga, gi, gu, ge, go*
The *sa* line hardened becomes *za, ji, zu, ze, zo*
The *ta* line hardened becomes *da, ji, dzu, de, do*

The *ha* line hardened becomes *ba, bi, bu, be, bo*
The *ha* line softened becomes *pa, pi, pu, pe, po*

ma	mi	mu	me	mo
ya		yu		yo
ra	ri	ru	re	ro
wa				(wo)
				o

Add *ya, yu* or *yo* to *ki, shi, chi, ni, hi, mi* and *ri*:

kya, kyu, kyo / gya, gyu, gyo
shya, shyu, shyo / jya, jyu, jyo
chya, chyu, chyo
nya, nyu, nyo
hya, hyu, hyo / bya, byu, byo / pya, pyu, pyo
mya, myu, myo
rya, ryu, ryo

One or two things to notice:

The syllables in blue are exceptions. In the *sa* line there is no *si* sound - it has been changed to *shi*. Likewise, in the *ta* line, *ti* and *tu* are changed. The *fu* in the *ha* line is a combination of "hu" and "fu" and sounds rather like our word "who" but with the mouth only a little bit open. The "r" of the *ra* line is pronounced almost like a "d" with the tongue behind the hard palate.

The *ya* line is missing a couple of sounds. They used to be there, but now what might be *yi* is just *i* and *ye* is just *e*.

"*Wa*" is more like "ooa" and the *wo* in brackets is now an *o* and is only used as an object marker (don't worry about it: we'll come to object markers later.)

You will notice that there is no 'L' sound - in Japanese it becomes an 'R': (try "Red lorry, yellow lorry" on a Japanese friend...). There is also no 'V' sound, so 'B' is substituted for foreign words such as "video" which becomes "bideo".

In general the emphasis in Japanese words is on the first syllable, although this isn't cast in stone. An example might be the girl's name *Tomoko* which would be <u>To</u>*moko* but in English might be *Tom<u>ō</u>ko*

Another thing to be aware of in the pronunciation of Japanese is long vowel sounds. Often in *hiragana* you just add another vowel, so instead of *ka* you have *kaa*. In the case of long 'o' sounds, they are sometimes *oo* or, more often, *ou*. It is important to know whether a vowel is long or short: *chīzu*, is 'cheese', whereas *chizu* is 'a map' - not much good if you are hungry.

If you need to show a double consonant in Japanese, you put a half-sized *tsu* in front of the consonant. In our writing system (*rōmaji*) it would look like this:

kakō	the mouth of a river	かこう
kakkō	a cuckoo	かっこう

A good point is that Japanese is pronounced exactly as it is written, unlike English:

> Walking through the rough woods near Slough, the pollen was enough to make me cough.
>
> I pre**sent**ed the mayor with a **pre**sent of a bottle of champagne.
>
> The **sus**pect looked at me sus**pic**iously.
>
> The nurse went back to the **ward** after**wards**.
>
> He had the nature of a mature person.
>
> I ate my steak on a table made of teak

And, as well, there are words in English which sound the same but which are written differently:

    Bare/bear   wail/whale   ceiling/sealing   sole/soul

    Tear(rip)/tear(cry)   tear(cry)/tier   spelled/spelt

    Pale/pail etc.

Be grateful if you were brought up speaking English and haven't had to learn it as a foreign language!

The next section is a short introduction to the Japanese writing system, with some charts to show the syllabary.

The Imperial Bridge, Nikko

The written language

The Japanese writing system is not quite as complicated as it appears once you know how it works.

I am going to America.

Watashi wa Amerika ni ikimasu.
[*rōmaji*]

わたし は あめりか に いきます。
[*hiragana*]

わたし は アメリカ に いきます。
[*katakana*]

私 は アメリカ に 行きます。
[*Kanji*]

Rōmaji (Roman letters) for all the sounds in Japanese, but not necessarily able to be understood by the Japanese themselves.

Hiragana for all the sounds in Japanese. In general use in combination with *katakana* and *Kanji*.

Katakana for all the sounds in Japanese. Used for foreign names and words, for names of birds, animals and flowers. Also used a lot in advertisements, hoardings etc. because its straight lines are easy to read quickly. Specific to *katakana* is that long vowels are shown by a line: デパート, *depāto*, a department store.

Kanji The picture characters borrowed from the Kan region of China. They often have several pronunciations (readings) and will also convey a meaning. They are often put together in combinations. For example 銀 is 'silver' and 行, as in the example sentence above, is to do with 'going'. Put together, 銀行 (*ginkō*) is a bank: 'silver to go'?? Generally if two *Kanji* characters are put together to form a word they will both be of Chinese origin, but sometimes two Japanese origin characters are put together in the same way.

The following page gives the *hiragana* and *katakana* syllabaries. There are practice charts at the end of the book which you are welcome to photocopy.

(Extra observant people will notice that " *wa*" is written as "*ha*" (は) – don't ask…)

Hiragana

あ a	い i	う u	え e	お o
か ka	き ki	く ku	け ke	こ ko
さ sa	し shi	す su	せ se	そ so
た ta	ち chi	つ tsu	て te	と to
な na	に ni	ぬ nu	ね ne	の no
は ha	ひ hi	ふ fu	へ he	ほ ho
ま ma	み mi	む mu	め me	も mo
や ya		ゆ yu		よ yo
ら ra	り ri	る ru	れ re	ろ ro
わ wa				を w/o
ん n				

Katakana

ア a	イ i	ウ u	エ e	オ o
カ ka	キ ki	ク ku	ケ ke	コ ko
サ sa	シ shi	ス su	セ se	ソ so
タ ta	チ chi	ツ tsu	テ te	ト to
ナ na	ニ ni	ヌ nu	ネ ne	ノ no
ハ ha	ヒ hi	フ fu	ヘ he	ホ ho
マ ma	ミ mi	ム mu	メ me	モ mo
ヤ ya		ユ yu		ヨ yo
ラ ra	リ ri	ル ru	レ re	ロ ro
ワ wa				ヲ w/o
ン n				

To harden the *ka, sa, ta, ha* lines add two little lines to the right of the character:

が ざ だ ば　　　ガ ザ ダ バ
ga za da ba　　ga za da ba

To soften the *ha* line add a little circle:

ぱ ぴ ぷ　　　パ ピ プ
pa pi pu　　　pa pi pu

Combination characters are written with the second character half-size, as follows:

しょ　　にゅ　　　ピュ　　ジェ
shyo　　nyu　　　pyu　　je

Below is an example of how written Japanese might look. The traditional way of writing is vertically from right to left, so books etc. are "backwards" to our eyes. Often, however, the horizontal form is also used, especially in combination with Western text (which is a bit difficult to read vertically!):

g
a
r
d
e
n

There are a number of points to notice:

1. The first section is written entirely in *hiragana,* with just ピーター (Peter - highlighted) in *katakana*.

    The second section is exactly the same text but using *Kanji*. This not only takes up less space on the page but it is much easier to read because the *Kanji* characters break it up.

2. There are no breaks between words, which is another reason why the *hiragana* version is more difficult to read. Sometimes you can't tell where one word ends and the next one begins. You can even start a word at the bottom of a column and finish it at the top of the next one.

3. Punctuation is limited. You don't, for example, need question marks because you have *ka* to indicate a question (see p.19). Full stops and commas are used, and quotation marks are shown by square brackets.

4. When you are writing Japanese, the order in which you do the strokes and the particular shape of each stroke is very important, so a great deal of practice is required!

5. You will notice in the third line of the *hiragana* two half-size characters (highlighted). The first one, つ, is to double the "s" of the *shi* after it (as mentioned on p.10). The second one, よ, is part of *shyō*, which, without the よ would just be *shi*.

これはわたしのくるまです。あかいです。たなかさんのくるまはあかくないで、くろいです。きのうのあめがふりましたから、たなかさんといっしょにくるまでおてらをみにいきました。「このおてらはとてもきれいです。」とたなかさんがいいました。おてらのなかで、ともだちのピーターさんにあいました。

これは私の車です。赤いです。田中さんの車は赤くないで、黒いです。きのう雨が降りましたから、田中さんと一緒に車でお寺を見に行きました。「このお寺はとても綺麗です。」と田中さんが言いました。お寺の中で、友達のピーターさんに会いました。

We are not really studying the writing system - just enough information as to how it works. If you are planning to learn to write these two syllabaries, you need to understand the stroke shapes and order.

The following are one or two helpful hints for remembering some of the characters:

1. *He* in both systems is the same, *ka* is nearly the same, and *ya* is quite similar.

    へ　へ　　　　か　カ　　　　　や　ヤ

2. In Hiragana, *ne, re* and *wa* all start in a similar way but finish differently.

    ね　れ　わ

3. In Hiragana, *ha* and *ho* are very similar.

    は　ほ

4. In Katakana *ni* and *mi* are derived from the Kanji for two and three.

    ニ　ミ

5. In Katakana *tsu, so* and *no* are all downward strokes with a lessening number of little lines beside them

    ツ　ソ　ノ

6. In Katakana *shi* and *n* are upward strokes with similar little lines.

    シ　ン

Chapter 1
- Basic grammar

Here is a sentence:

Watashi wa sensei desu. I am a teacher.

Watashi means "I" but also (with a different pronunciation) means "private", which is quite apt.

Wa is the topic marker, showing that I am the topic of the sentence. *Wa* is one of several Japanese post-positional particles, which sound scary but which are fine once you get used to them.

Sensei means "teacher" - easy!

Desu for our purposes at present is a verb meaning "is". Actually, it is a copula (basically a connecting word), but you needn't worry about it: treat it as a verb.

If you were introducing yourself in Japanese, you could say *Watashi wa* [name] *desu* but normally, unless you particularly want to emphasize that it is you called [name] and not someone else, you can just say [name] *desu* and it will be perfectly clear to the listener because it is you who are speaking.

Affirmative and negative, past and present

Affirmative and negative are the same as positive and negative in English. Past and present are slightly more complicated. There is only one form of the past tense of any verb which sounds very limiting, but you are perfectly able to convey what might be the perfect tense ("I went") or imperfect tense ("I was going") by the use of extra words modifying the verb.

What we call the present tense is, in Japanese, the non-past. That is to say the same verb form will serve for present and future action. It is not unlike English in that if you say "I am going for a walk" it could be that you are either in the process of going for a walk or you are planning to go for a walk at some future time. You would need to modify the sentence to make it quite clear.

Is and is not

We have already seen that *desu* means "is". When you say the word, you don't pronounce the final "u", so it sounds like "des".

De wa arimasen means "is not".

Practice 1 (a)

Using *desu* or *de wa arimasen*, put in the right ending to make each sentence correct:

1. *pen*_____

2. *futobōru*_____

3. *orenji* _____

4. *hottodoggu*_____

5. *banana*_____

Was and was not

Deshita means "was" and *de wa arimasen deshita* means "was not". Notice that *de wa arimasen deshita* is a logical combination of negative and past.

TO BE OR NOT TO BE

Non-past		Past	
Positive	Negative	Positive	Negative
desu is	**de wa arimasen** is not	**deshita** was	**de wa arimasen deshita** was not

Practice 1 (b)

Put in the correct form of the verb so the sentences make sense.

1. *Tokei (watch)* ....

2. *Yūrei (ghost)* ....

3. *Basu* ....

4. *Tanaka san deshita ka.* (Was that Mr. Tanaka?)

   Iie, (No) *Tanaka san* ....

   Yamada san ....

Useful notes

a) You will see from No. 4 above that Mr. Tanaka is *Tanaka san*. The first important point is that the family name is used on more formal occasions rather than the given name. (This can lead to complications if you are with a family all sharing the same family name…) It is typical of Japanese culture that the group is more important than the individual, so the use of the family name is, to some extent, an example of this.

Japanese names usually have the family name first, so Tanaka Yoshida and his wife, Tanaka Haruko, though in the West Japanese names are beginning to be quoted with the given name first.

San is a suffix applied to male or female names - so Mr., Mrs. or Miss - and is used most commonly in ordinary conversation. The other suffixes are:

Chan for small children and young girls
Kun for young boys
Sama for someone of a higher rank than the speaker, such as the President of the company or one of the gods.

If, for example, you have grown up with someone you called ……*chan* when you were little, you would probably go on calling her that as you both got older: you wouldn't change to ……*san*. You <u>never</u> use these suffixes after your own name.

b) Also from No. 4 above, you will notice *iie* meaning "no". "Yes" in Japanese is *hai*. There are two things to make a note of here:

   1. *Iie* can be quite abrupt and even rude. It can certainly be used in, for instance: "Is your phone number 6032?" "No, it's 6042." But possibly the answer to "Are you going to the party on Saturday?" might have to be "Unfortunately, I am unable to go because the circumstances are …."

   2. *Hai* actually means "You are right" which can lead to misunderstanding.

      I was out at a park with a Japanese friend and I asked her "You haven't been here before, have you?" An English person would say "No, I haven't", but my friend answered "*Hai...*" meaning "You are right. I haven't been here before."

c) Again, from No. 4 above, one sentence ends in *ka*. This indicates that it is a question. *Tanaka san deshita ka.* Was it Mr. Tanaka? *Tanaka san deshita.* It was Mr. Tanaka.

Chapter 2
- Borrowed words

You will have noticed from the first *desu* exercise that the nouns used are all English words although mostly spelled differently to fit with Japanese pronunciation. There are many so-called "borrowed words" in Japanese. One reason for this is that the country was closed to the outside world for 250 years until the second half of the 19th century. When foreigners started coming back to Japan, there were many objects and expressions for which the Japanese had no equivalent so they adopted whatever language they found them in. In Japanese these are called *gai rai go*, language coming from overseas. Of course, English also has many borrowed words - for example, café, restaurant, verandah, shampoo, alligator, barbecue etc. These foreign origin words slide into the language and become part of it.

Practice 2 (a)

Try working out what these words are. Remember to say them with Japanese pronunciation:

bōto _____

tākī _____

erebētā _____

sōsēji _____

bōru _____

rekōdo _____

kurarinetto _____

naifu _____

suchuwādesu _____

intabyū _____

Practice 2 (b)

Match the following borrowed words with the appropriate picture:

(cake and rolling pin image)	kēki / kōhī	(bottle and glass image)
(supermarket shelves image)	konpyūtā / sandoitchi	(people dancing image)
(bus image)	bēsubōru	
	terebi / pātei	(birthday cake image)
(carrot image)	rajio	
(cup of coffee image)	basu / chyokoreito	(radio image)
	uain	(sandwich image)
(computer image)	aisukurīmu	
(chocolate bar image)	sūpā	(television image)

Chapter 3
- Greetings and Introductions

Greetings

It is useful to have a grasp of greeting words - particularly to make a good first impression... Here are some basic expressions:

o-hayō gozaimasu*	Good morning - up to 10.00 am (although you don't have to check your watch!)
kon nichi wa	Hello, good day *Nichi* means 'day'.
kon ban wa	Good evening *Ban* means 'evening'.
o-yasumi nasai*	Good night *Yasumi* is a rest or a holiday, so this is literally 'Please have an honourable rest'.
sayōnara	Goodbye

*The prefix, *o-*, is a so-called honorific, used to make the expression more polite and formal. *Gozaimasu* is the more polite form of *desu*. To a friend you would probably just say '*o-hayō*'.

Bowing

The traditional way of greeting someone in Japan is by bowing. Men bow with their arms at their sides and women with their hands held together in front of them. Westerners are advised to restrict themselves to a nod of the head or be prepared to shake hands. The complexities of bowing are infinite. If an underling bows to someone his senior, he must make sure that his bow is lower than that of his superior and that he doesn't straighten up from it until his superior has finished bowing.

Introductions

This is some appropriate vocabulary for use in introductions:

kochira wa.....	This is.....
hajimemashite	How do you do?
dōzo yoroshiku	I'm pleased to meet you.
yoroshiku o-negaishimasu	I'm pleased to meet you too.

The following could be a typical introductory scene:

Kon nichi wa.

Kon nichi wa.

Kochira wa Tanakasan desu.

Suzuki desu. Hajimemashite.

Hajimemashite. Dōzo yoroshiku.

Yoroshiku o-negaishimasu.

Business cards

Business cards are very important in Japan. As a visitor you will be given one at every turn. Often Japanese business cards are printed in Japanese on one side and in English on the other. Formerly (it may not be so easy now) a Japanese person could look at someone else's business card and, judging by their position in a particular company, would have a fair idea of what school and university they went to.

```
Pretence University
3-9-14 Minami-azabu
Minato-ku
Tokyo
Telephone:
Email:
        Tanaka Shigeru
  Professor of Japanese Literature
```

```
見せかけた　大学
東京港区南麻布3-9-14

電話：
メイル：

        田中茂
    日本文学教授
```

Practice 3

Translate this conversation into Japanese:

Good evening.

Good evening.

This is Miss Shimizu.

I am (Miss) Takahashi. I'm pleased to meet you.

I am pleased to meet you too.

Please and thank you

While we are on the subject of greetings and introductions, let us look at "please" and "thank you". There are different degrees of politeness and formality:

Please

dōzo	In answer to "May I use this pen?" "Yes, do." When giving something to someone: "Here is the book you asked for." Letting someone go in front of you
kudasai	Asking for something in a shop Asking someone to do something (a polite order - not for asking a superior to do something!)
o-negai shimasu	More polite: someone doing you a favour: "Shall I open the window?" "Would you like some tea?"

Thank you

dōmo	"Thanks" (casual)
arigatō	I'm going out: your supper's in the oven.
dōmo arigatō	Your supper's ready and I've made a cake.
arigatō gozaimasu	Your supper's ready, I've made a cake and bought a bottle of wine.
arigatō gozaimashita	Here is your birthday present. It was very expensive!
dōmo arigatō gozaimasu	Even though I'm your boss and much superior to you, I've sent that report on your behalf.
dōmo arigatō gozaimashita	We are making you President of the company with a salary increase of ¥ umpteen a year.
dōitashimashite	Don't mention it.

Chapter 4
- Nationality and Language

It is possible, especially as a foreigner in Japan, that someone might ask you your nationality, or it is mentioned in the introduction process. The suffix to denote nationality is ~*jin*, meaning "person", attached to the name of the country. In English we use "Japanese", "French" etc. for both the language and the nationality.
In Japanese there is a different suffix, *go*, to denote the language.

Nihon jin	Japanese person	*Nihon go*	Japanese language
Amerika jin	American person	*Amerika go*	American language
Itaria jin	Italian person	*Itaria go*	Italian language
Furansu jin	French person	*Furansu go*	French language
Chūgoku jin	Chinese person	*Chūgoku go*	Chinese language
Igirisu jin	English person	*Ei go* **(NB)**	English language

England was formerly *Eikoku* so *Eikoku jin* could be used. You still come across it sometimes today. *Ei go* is obviously related to this.

You will also find that *Igirisu* can refer to the United Kingdom, not just England.

Doitsu jin	German person	*Doitsu go*	German language

The word for "German" in Japanese copies the sound of "Deutsch".

Practice 4

What would these be?   *Burajiru jin*   *Sukottorando jin*   *Uēruzu jin*

Supein go   *Roshia go*   *Oranda go*

Mr. Smith is an American, M. Dupont is French. Their common language is Japanese (unlikely as it may sound), so introduce them to each other.

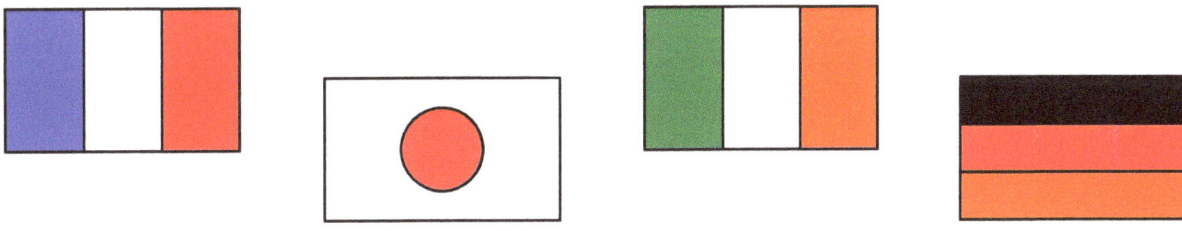

Chapter 5
- Belonging

We mentioned post-positional particles on p. 16, with *wa* being the topic marker. Another useful particle is *no* which indicates possession. It can be used simply as in *Watashi no kōhi desu* - It's my coffee, or *Tanaka san no futobōru dewa arimasen* - It isn't Mr. Tanaka's football.

It is also used to identify someone by their company: *Mitsubishi no Tanaka desu* - I am Tanaka from Mitsubishi.

Translate the following introductory sentence:

Kochira wa Robatsu san desu. Robatsu san wa City Insurance *no Igirisu jin desu.*

(We can't, of course, tell whether *Robatsu san* is male or female from this sentence…)

No can also be used to denote where something or someone comes from:

Amerika no aisu kurīmu desu.   *Tōkyo no Asada san desu.*
It's American ice cream.   It's Mr./Mrs./Miss Asada from Tokyo.

Practice 5

Translate these conversations into Japanese:

Suzuki:	Good morning, Mr. Tanaka.
Tanaka:	Good morning. This is Mr. Fisher from Ireland.
Fisher:	How do you do? I'm pleased to meet you.
Suzuki:	I'm pleased to meet you too.

Hiroshi kun:	It's my pen.
Sachiko chan:	No, it's my pen.
Sensei:	Good morning. It's mine. Thank you.

You might have wondered why they are called post-positional particles. It's because they always come directly after the word they are referring to.

Chapter 6
- Numbers

Counting in Japanese is not quite as easy as in English, but we shall start with basic numbers and come to the more difficult ones later on.

0	zero/rei
1	ichi
2	ni
3	san
4	shi/yon These are both 4, but there are times when one is more appropriate.
5	go
6	roku
7	shichi/nana These are both 7, but etc. etc.
8	hachi
9	kyū/ku The pronunciation of 9 and 10 depends on what follows each number.
10	jyū/jyu
11	jyū ichi
12	jyū ni
13	jyū san
14	jyū shi/jyū yon
15	jyū go
16	jyū roku
17	jyū shichi/jyū nana
18	jyū hachi
19	jyū kyū
20	ni jyū
21	ni jyū ichi
31	san jyū ichi
99	kyū jyū kyū
100	hyaku

These might help you to remember the numbers 1 to 10:

ichi

ni

san

shi

go

roku

shichi

hachi

kyū

jyū

Telephone numbers (denwa bangō)

These use the numbers above, and *zero, yon* and *nana* rather than the alternatives.

The gap between the code and the number is *no*, belonging to.

0248 - 537 691 = *zero ni yon hachi no go san nana roku kyū ichi*

Work out what your own telephone number would be.

Practice 6 (a)

Try these sums:

6 + 7 = _____   84 - 30 = _____

17 x 4 = _____   108 divided by 9 = _____

Translate: Mr. Suzuki's telephone number is 03-4798-6521

You might be interested in the fact that *denwa*, meaning telephone, is written 電話 which literally means "electric conversation".

Bigger numbers

Notice variations in pronunciation:

100	hyaku	百	1,000	sen	千	10,000	ichiman	万
200	nihyaku		2,000	nisen		100,000	jyūman	
300	sanbyaku		3,000	sanzen		1,000,000	hyakuman	
400	yonhyaku		4,000	yonsen		10,000,000	senman	
500	gohyaku		5,000	gosen		100,000,000	ichioku	
600	roppyaku		6,000	rokusen		1,000,000,000	jyūoku	
700	nanahyaku		7,000	nanasen		10,000,000,000	hyakuoku	
800	happyaku		8,000	hassen		100,000,000,000	sen'oku	
900	kyūhyaku		9,000	kyūsen		1,000,000,000,000	itchō	

Notice the unit of *man*, 10,000. It can cause some brain-stretching, especially for non-mathematical people! 46,000 would be *yon man roku sen*.

Ikura desu ka.   How much is it?

Yen, the national currency of Japan, written ¥ for short, is often pronounced *en*.

Practice 6 (b)

Shinbun wa ikura desu ka.
Hyaku yon jyū en desu.   ¥ 140

Tokei wa ikura desuka.

¥ 35,700

Kuruma wa ikura desu ka.

   ¥ 8,200,000

Hon wa ikura desu ka.   ¥ 695

What would these numbers be in Japanese?

3,560   18,685   420,799

Kanji numbers

To give you a start on writing Kanji numbers, here are the numbers 1 to 10:

1	2	3	4	5
一	二	三	四	五

6	7	8	9	10
六	七	八	九	十

With many thanks to Nihon Ichiban for the use of their Kanji numbers.

Shopping Mall, Takamatsu

Counters

In English some nouns are countable and some uncountable. For example, we cannot say "three breads" - we have to specify "three loaves of bread" or "three slices of bread". We can, however, say "three friends". In Japanese all nouns are countable and there are many "counters" with which to count them. Some of the counters are very odd - why should the counter for a 'cello be the same as for a mirror, a page in a newspaper, a pool or a tennis court? There is one counter for large animals and a different one for small animals, although where the line of distinction is drawn is anyone's guess.

The following is a list of the most usual counters and the things they are used for:

hiki   small animals

hai   glass - or cupfuls

hon   cylindrical objects - pencils, bananas, trees, bottles, computer programs (!)

soku   pairs - shoes, socks etc.

satsu bound things - books, magazines

dai   machines - cars etc.

mai   flat, thin things - postcards, sheets of paper, T-shirts etc.

Confused statue at Miyajima

It is unlikely that even the Japanese know all the counters, but several of them are used regularly - see below. The first column contains the default counters which are used for concrete, inanimate or abstract nouns for which no other counter exists. Notice the changes in pronunciation depending on the number to which the counter is attached.

		hiki	*hai*	*hon*
1.	hitotsu	ippiki	ippai	ippon
2.	futatsu	nihiki	nihai	nihon
3.	mittsu	sanbiki	sanbai	sanbon
4.	yottsu	yonhiki	yonhai	yonhon
5.	itsutsu	gohiki	gohai	gohon
6.	muttsu	roppiki	roppai	roppon
7.	nanatsu	nanahiki	nanahai	nanahon
8.	yattsu	happiki	happai	happon
9.	kokonotsu	kyūhiki	kyūhai	kyūhon
10.	tō	jyūhiki	jyūhai	jyūhon
11.	jyūichi	jyūippiki	jyūippai	jyūippon
How many?	ikutsu	nanbiki	nanbai	nanbon

	soku	*satsu*	*dai*	*mai*
1.	issoku	issatsu	ichidai	ichimai
2.	nisoku	nisatsu	nidai	nimai
3.	sanzoku	sansatsu	sandai	sanmai
4.	yonsoku	yonsatsu	yondai	yonmai
5.	gosoku	gosatsu	godai	gomai
6.	rokusoku	rokusatsu	rokudai	rokumai
7.	nanasoku	nanasatsu	nanadai	nanamai
8.	hassoku	hassatsu	hachidai	hachimai
9.	kyūsoku	kyūsatsu	kyūdai	kyūmai
10.	jyūsoku	jyūsatsu	jyūdai	jyūmai
11.	jyūissoku	jyūissatsu	jyūichidai	jyūichimai
How many?	nanzoku	nansatsu	nandai	nanmai

Watashi wa kuruma ga nidai arimasu.
I have two cars.

Banana o sanbon tabemashita.
I ate three bananas.

kudasai is "please", so asking for something in a shop would be:

Object, particle, amount, counter, please:

Shinbun o ni mai kudasai. Two newspapers please.

Practice 6 (c)

Ask for these things:

Five pairs of socks [*kutsu shita*].

Three books.

One cup of coffee.

Two T-shirts

Four cats

Chapter 7
- This and that, here and there

The *ko/so/a/do* system

	ko- series near speaker	**so-** series near listener	**a-** series away from speaker and listener	**do-** series question word (plus *ka*)
Pronoun	**kore** this	**sore** that	**are** that over there	**dore** - which? of more than 2 things
Demonstrative adjective	**kono** + noun this thing	**sono** + noun that thing	**ano** + noun that thing over there	**dono** + noun which thing?
Adverb	**koko** here	**soko** there	**asoko** over there	**doko** where?
Formal for **kore** etc. Informal: used only in speech	**kochira** this/here **kochi**	**sochira** that/there **sochi**	**achira** that over there/ over there **achi**	**dochira** - which? of 2 things **dochi**

kore   *sono hon*

ano hon

dono hon

1. All these words are stand-alone except *kono, sono, ano* and *dono* which can never stand alone.

Kore wa pen desu. This is a pen. *Sore wa watashi no desu.* That's mine.

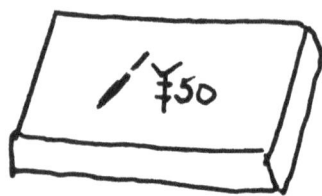  

Ano pen wa ikura desuka. How much is that pen over there?
Ano pen wa ¥50 desu. That pen is ¥50.

2. In the section on introductions we used *kochira wa* for "this is". This series can also be used for place:

Dōzo kochira e. Please come this way.

e is another post positional particle indicating direction. We will deal with it later on.

3. In the *do-* series, note the difference between *dore* and *dochira*, and, of course, as question words they need *ka* at the end of the sentence.

Basu wa doko desu ka. Where is the bus?

Practice 7

Fill in the gaps with the appropriate word:

1. *Sore wa ikura desu ka.* _____ *wa ¥98 desu.*

2. *Kono tokei wa Nihon no desu ka. Iie* _____ *tokei wa Amerika no desu.*

and translate the following:

> *Resutoran wa doko desuka.*
>
> *Dono resutoran desuka.*
>
> *Ano Chūgoku no resutoran desu.*
>
> *Aa! Are wa asoko desu.*

Chapter 8
- Question words

So far, apart from the *do-* series above, we have only had *ikura* and *ikutsu* as interrogative words. Now for some more.

dare/donata	who?	*Tanaka san wa dare desu ka.* Who is Mr. Tanaka? *Nihon jin desu.* He is a Japanese person.
nan/nani	what?	*Kore wa nan desu ka.* What is this?
itsu	when?	*Tanjōbi wa itsu desu ka.* When is your birthday?
ikura	how much?	*Kamera wa ikura desu ka. ¥50,000 desu.* How much is the camera? It's ¥50,000.
ikutsu	how many?	*Orenji wa ikutsu arimasu ka.* How many oranges are there?

Notes

1. *Dare* is less formal than *donata*.

2. *Nani* when it's on it's own but *nan* if it's before another word:

    [*Nani?*]   "What (did you say)?"

    Nan desu ka.   What is it?

3. From this list, *dare/donata*, *nan/nani*, (and *dore* and *dochira* from the previous list) cannot take *wa* as a topic marker but have to take *ga* instead. REMEMBER THIS!

Also *ga* must be used in the answer:

  Dare ga kimashita ka.   Who came?

  Tanaka san ga kimashita.   Mr. Tanaka came.

Practice 8

Translate these sentences:

a) This is a book.

b) That over there is not a car.   (If it's not a car, what on earth is it??)

c) Where is the camera? It's here.

d) Which one [of many] was it?

e) *Sore/are wa hana desuka.*

f) *Dono ie desu ka.*

g) *Shima wa doko desu ka. Asoko desu.*

h) *Kono inu wa watashi no de wa arimasen.*

Shrine Guardian, Nikko

The Great Buddha, Kamakura

Chapter 9
- Post positional particles so far

We have mentioned these so far:

wa   Topic marker. It can be thought of as "as for".

Watashi wa Amerika jin dewa arimasen.
As for me, I'm not American.

Kono tokei wa Nihon no desu.
As for this watch, it's Japanese.

ka   Question marker. It always comes at the end of a sentence.

Achira wa dare desu ka.
Who is that over there?

no   Belonging

Tanaka san no shinbun.
Mr. Tanaka's newspaper

ga   Subject marker after some question words.

Dare ga ikimashita ka.
Who went?
Furansu jin ga ikimashita.
A/the French person went.

The advantage of all these particles is that the order of the words in a sentence really doesn't matter providing the main verb comes at the end. The particle indicates the function of the previous word.

This is a good example:

The particle *o* which used to be *wo* is an object marker.

Inu wa neko o mimashita.
The dog saw the cat.

Neko wa inu o mimashita.
The cat saw the dog.

Inu o neko wa mimashita.
Who saw whom?

Two other common particles which will be useful are *e* and *ni*. *E* we had on page 36 in the phrase, *Dōzo kochira e* and it means "to/in the direction of". When it comes to the writing system, you will note that *e* is written *he*. *E* and *ni* both mean "[going] to", but *ni* is more specific:

> I am going to school
> Gakkō *ni* ikimasu.
>
> I am going to Tokyo.
> Tōkyō *e* ikimasu.

Ni has a number of other meanings which we shall deal with later.

The last particle for now is *de* which is "by means of", so:

I am writing in Japanese.	Nihongo de kakimasu.
I am writing with a pen.	Pen de kakimasu.
How are you going to school?	Nan de gakkō ni ikimasu ka.

Practice 9

Insert the correct particle in the gaps:

1. This is my car.   Kore .... watashi .... kuruma desu.

2. Who is coming?   Dare .... kimasuka.

3. Did you come by bicycle?   Jitensha .... kimashitaka.

4. That is Mr. Tanaka's watch. Sore .... Tanaka san no tokei desu.

5. Please show me that camera. Sono kamera .... misete kudasai.

Chapter 10
- Dates and days

| *ototoi* | *kinō* | *kyō* | *asu/ashita* | *asatte* |
| day before yesterday | yesterday | today | tomorrow | day after tomorrow |

Years

kyo nen 去年　　　　*kotoshi* 今年　　　　*rai nen* 来年
last year　　　　　　this year (the "now" year)　　next year (the coming year)
(the past year)　　　今 *kon* or *ima* means "now"　　来る *kuru* means "to come"

Notice that the character for "year" is read as *nen* or *toshi* depending on the context.

What year?　*nan nen*　何年

Months

January	*ichi gatsu*	一月	July	*shichi gatsu*	七月
February	*ni gatsu*	二月	August	*hachi gatsu*	八月
March	*san gatsu*	三月	September	*ku gatsu*	九月
April	*shi gatsu*	四月	October	*jū gatsu*	十月
May	*go gatsu*	五月	November	*jū ichi gatsu*	十一月
June	*roku gatsu*	六月	December	*jū ni gatsu*	十二月

What month?　*nan gatsu*　何月

Months are easy:　月 is moon, so they are the first moon, second moon etc.

Weeks

sen shū 先週　　　　*kon shū* 今週　　　　*rai shū* 来週
先 *sen* or *saki* means　this week　　　　　the coming week
"previous" or "past"

Which week?　*dono shū*　どの週

Dates

1st	*tsuitachi*	一日	11th	*jū ichi nichi*	十一日	21st	*ni jū ichi nichi*	二十一日
2nd	*futsuka*	二日	12th	*jū ni nichi*	十二日	22nd	*ni jū ni nichi*	二十二日
3rd	*mikka*	三日	13th	*jū san nichi*	十三日	23rd	*ni jū san nichi*	二十三日
4th	*yokka*	四日	14th	*jū yokka*	十四日	24th	*ni jū yokka*	二十四日
5th	*itsuka*	五日	15th	*jū go nichi*	十五日	25th	*ni jū go nichi*	二十五日
6th	*muika*	六日	16th	*jū roku nichi*	十六日	26th	*ni jū roku nichi*	二十六日
7th	*nanoka*	七日	17th	*jū shichi nichi*	十七日	27th	*ni jū shichi nichi*	二十七日
8th	*yōka*	八日	18th	*jū hachi nichi*	十八日	28th	*ni jū hachi nichi*	二十八日
9th	*kokonoka*	九日	19th	*jū kyū nichi*	十九日	29th	*ni jū kyū nichi*	二十九日
10th	*tōka*	十日	20th	*hatsuka*	二十日	30th	*san jū nichi*	三十日

What date?   *nan nichi*   何日

Notice the underlined dates which have a different pronunciation from what you might expect. A particular note should be made of the 4th and 8th, which the Japanese think all foreigners get wrong…

Days

Monday	*getsu yōbi*	月曜日	moon day
Tuesday	*ka yōbi*	火曜日	fire day
Wednesday	*sui yōbi*	水曜日	water day
Thursday	*moku yōbi*	木曜日	wood day
Friday	*kin yōbi*	金曜日	gold/money day
Saturday	*do yōbi*	土曜日	earth day
Sunday	*nichi yōbi*	日曜日	sun day

What day?   *nan yōbi*   何曜日

月 as in 一月 but with a different reading - means "the moon"

日 has several readings: *nichi, jitsu, hi* (hence *yōbi*) - means "day" or "sun"

曜日   曜 = day of the week, also "light" or "shine"

Notice what the days mean: Sunday and Monday are the same as ours.
Friday 金 - money (payday?)

> **Time**
>
> ~ ji ~時   ichi ji, ni ji etc.   half past one   ichi ji han   一時半
>   o'clock
>
> Watch out for 4.00 which is *yo ji* not *yon ji* as you might expect.

What time?   nan ji   何時

> **Minutes**
>
> | | | |
> |---|---|---|
> | ippun | 一分 | いっぷん |
> | ni-fun | 二分 | にふん |
> | san-pun | 三分 | さんぷん |
> | yon-pun | 四分 | よんぷん |
> | go-fun | 五分 | ごふん |
> | roppun | 六分 | ろっぷん |
> | nana-fun | 七分 | ななふん |
> | happun | 八分 | はっぷん |
> | kyū-fun | 九分 | きゅうふん |
> | juppun | 十分 | じゅっぷん |
> | jūippun | 十一分 | じゅういっぷん |
> | jūni-fun | 十二分 | じゅうにふん |
> | etc. | | |

The post positional particle for dates, days and time is *ni*, so "in the Spring" is *haru ni*, "on Sunday" is *nichiyōbi ni*, and "at 5 o'clock" is *go ji ni*.

Practice 10

When dealing with a date, the largest thing always comes first: year, month, day, time:

二千十五年三月十七日水曜日三時半。

Can you work out what this is?

Translate these sentences:

1. Today is 14th November.
2. Tomorrow will be 1st August.
3. Yesterday was 20th May.
4. The day after tomorrow will be Saturday, 27th December.
5. The day before yesterday was Thursday.

The Japanese for "birthday" is *tanjōbi*, so how would you say "My birthday is [on] ……….(date)."?

Toshogu Shrine, Nikko

Seasons

It seems appropriate to mention the seasons here. They are:

Spring *Haru*	Autumn *Aki*

Summer *Natsu*	Winter *Fuyu*

Because Japan is a very long, thin country, the climate varies a great deal from north to south.

The snow starts in October in Hokkaidō, the northernmost island, and works its way southwards. The same applies to the marvellous autumn colouring. When it is at its best in the north, it won't reach the south for some time. The so-called *sakura sen,* the "cherry blossom line" is the opposite, starting in the south and progressing upwards.

The seasons in Japan are similar to those in England. Each one is very distinct, but Japan has a much greater degree of humidity than Europe, especially at the height of summer. June is the month for very heavy rainfall.

It is well known that because Japan is resting on four tectonic plates, the country suffers from volcanic eruptions, earthquakes and tsunamis.

Japanese Geography

The name of the country, Japan, in Japanese is *Nihon* (日本), which means "Sun origin". The sun goddess gave birth to the islands of Japan and their national flag reflects this. The flag used before the second world war was the "Rising Sun":

A flag similar to this is still used by the naval defence force, but since 1945 the standard national flag of Japan has been:

A large proportion of the country is mountainous which means that housing tends to be crowded in those parts where building is possible. Because of the frequency of earthquakes, tall buildings have to contain steel in their walls so that they sway with the quake rather than resist it and collapse. It doesn't feel very pleasant if you are in one of these buildings, but it is much safer.

Chapter 11
- Verbs

As mentioned in the basic grammar section, there are three groups of verbs in Japanese. The table below gives some idea of how they work.

Meaning	Dictionary form	Non-past		Past	
		Positive	Negative	Positive	Negative
GROUP I[1]					
to write	kak-u	kak-imasu	kak-imasen	kak-imashita	kak-imasen deshita
to hurry	isog-u	isog-imasu	isog-imasen	isog-imashita	isog-imasen deshita
to drink	nom-u	nom-imasu	nom-imasen	nom-imashita	nom-imasen deshita
to die[2]	shin-u	shin-imasu	shin-imasen	shin-imashita	shin-imasen deshita
to call	yob-u	yob-imasu	yob-imasen	yob-imashita	yob-imasen deshita
to return	kaer-u	kaer-imasu	kaer-imasen	kaer-imashita	kaer-imasen deshita
to wait	mats-u	mach-imasu	mach-imasen	mach-imashita	mach-imasen deshita
to use	tsuka-u[3]	tsuka-imasu	tsuka-imasen	tsuka-imashita	tsuka-imasen deshita
to speak	hanas-u	hanash-imasu	hanash-imasen	hanash-imashita	hanash-imasen deshita
GROUP II[4]					
to eat	tabe-ru	tabe-masu	tabe-masen	tabe-mashita	tabe-masen deshita
to open	ake-ru	ake-masu	ake-masen	ake-mashita	ake-masen deshita
to see	mi-ru	mi-masu	mi-masen	mi-mashita	mi-masen deshita
to be	i-ru	i-masu	i-masen	i-mashita	i-masen deshita
GROUP III	Only two verbs				
to come	kuru	ki-masu	ki-masen	ki-mashita	ki-masen deshita
to do	suru	shimasu	shi-masen	shi-mashita	shi-masen deshita

1   These change their vowels according to what follows, i.e., ka**u**, ka**i**masu, ka**a**nai, ka**ite** etc.
2   The only verb ending in ~nu
3   This counts as *tsukaw-* so ending in a consonant
4   These keep their ~i or ~e ending whatever follows, i.e., **tabe**ru, **tabe**masu, **tabe**nai, **tabe**te etc.

The "dictionary form" is similar to what we would call the infinitive. It is what you would look up in a dictionary. There is no verb in Japanese which does not fit these patterns. Try declining these: the answers are in the answer section.

Group I	Group II
kesu - to turn off	*ageru* - to give
yomu - to read	*miseru* - to show
oyogu - to swim	*shimeru* - to shut
itadaku - to accept	*oriru* - to get off
motsu - to have/hold	*dekiru* - to be able
chigau - to be wrong	*hajimeru* - to begin
gambaru - to do one's best	*shiru* - to know
oyobu - to last	*susumeru* - to advance

Practice 11

Now we can try some proper sentences. Try translating these:

1. I am writing to (*ni*) Mr. Yamada.

2. My dog swam in (*de* in this case - don't ask!) the pool (*pūru*) today.

3. I waited for the bus but (*ga*) [it] didn't come.
   (NB *matsu*, to wait, takes a direct object, unlike in English. Think of "await", which does take a direct object.)

4. Mr. Suzuki went to Yokohama on the 14th.

5. Do you drink *sake*?

1. *Eigo de, "shiru" wa nan desu ka.*

2. *Dōa* (door) *o akemasen ka.*

3. *Endo san ni Amerika no kamera o misemashita.*

4. *Suzuki san wa kinō kēki o tabemasen deshita.*

5. *Hiroshi kun wa Nihon go de hanashimashita. Wakarimasen deshita.*
   (*wakaru* - to understand).

# Chapter 12
- Coming and Going

These verbs need some explanation and practice:

Iku to go   *kuru* to come   *kaeru* to return

Iku and *kuru* are very literal. In English you can invite someone to "come" on an outing with you, but in Japanese you can only come to wherever you are at that moment. Therefore you would say "Will you go with me to the beach next week?"

If you are speaking on the phone (or corresponding by email etc.), you cannot say "I will come to your office on Monday". It has to be "I will go..." So the conversation could be "What time will you come?" "I will go at 4.00."

Kaeru, as it says above is to return. It can mean returning to where you are at present, but it can also mean that you are returning to your home country from abroad.

An example: A Japanese boy on my doorstep was going back to Japan that evening, but before he left he had to go off and collect something for the journey. I said "What time will you return?" meaning what time would he be back at my house. His reply was "6.00" which was the time of his flight back to Japan.

Iku and *kaeru* decline normally, but *kuru* is a Group III verb, so you will need to look back and see how it declines.

Practice 12 (a)   Fill in the chart below:

Meaning	Dictionary form	Non-past		Past	
		Positive	Negative	Positive	Negative
to go					
to come					
to return					

Practice 12 (b)

Translate these sentences:

1. [I] will go tomorrow.

2. Mr. Tanaka came yesterday.

3. Mr. Yamada is returning to Tokyo.

4. [I] went to Japan last year.

5. [He] came back yesterday.

6. Mr. Tanaka did not go to the Embassy. (*taishikan*)

7. [I] won't come back next year.

8. [He] didn't come last week.

9. [He] didn't come back from (*kara*) France.

10. Mr. Suzuki is not going to Germany today.

11. Are [you] coming tomorrow?

12. Where are [you] going? To a meeting. (*kaigi*)

Note

Pronouns in square brackets are omitted in Japanese. It is usually obvious from the context who the relevant person is. If you are talking to someone, you generally do not call them "you" but address them by their name (family or given) or their position - doctor, teacher etc. - or look them in the eye so they know you are talking to them.

Means of transport

Remember that on page 42 the post positional particle *de* was given as "by means of". This also applies to methods of transport. For example:

Densha de Tokyo ni ikimasu.   I am going to Tokyo by train.

Nan de kimasuka   How are you coming?
Kuruma de kimasu.   I am coming by car.

Chapter 13
- Existence and fact

In English we have existence: to be, and possession: to have. Japanese is slightly different.

There is a shop over there. *Asoko ni mise ga arimasu.*

Mr. Tanaka is over there.   *Asoko ni Tanaka san ga imasu.*

So the difference between *aru* and *iru* is that *aru* is used for inanimate objects and *iru* for animate objects. Mnemonic: **a**ru for **i**nanimate, **i**ru for **a**nimate.

(When I asked a Japanese person which verb to use for a dead animal, she reckoned it was still *iru*…)

But, of course, we have already had *desu* which we took to mean "is".

Notice the difference between these two sentences:

Asoko ni mise ga arimasu.   There is a shop over there.

Mise wa Chūgoku no desu.   The shop is Chinese.

Desu is used for a factual statement, *aru* and *iru* for existence.

Just to complicate things, *aru* is also used as "to have", as in *Tokei ga arimasu* - I have a watch. *Aru* takes *ga* in this usage.

Declension of *aru* and *iru*

These follow the normal pattern of verb declension:

is	is not	was	was not
arimasu imasu	arimasen imasen	arimashita imashita	arimasen deshita imasen deshita

Note

ga is used as the subject marker in some of these sentences because they are random statements. In the second examples, *mise* **ga** *arimasu* means "there is **a** shop", whereas *mise* **wa** means "**the** shop", which has already been mentioned.

Practice 13

Fill in the gaps with the appropriate verb. <u>Note</u> that *ni* in these sentences means "in". (We did mention on page 42 that there would be other uses of *ni*....)

1. *Tanaka san ga daidokoro ni* .... (arimasu/imasu)

2. *Neko ga niwa ni* .... (arimasu/imasu/desu)

3. *Shokudō ni e ga* .... (arimasu/imasu)

4. *Yamada san no uchi wa Tokyo ni* ..... (arimasu/imasu)

5. *Kore wa nan* .... (arimasuka/desuka/imasuka)

6. *Ano hon wa akai* .... (arimasu/desu)

Translate these sentences into Japanese:

1. Mr. Tanaka wasn't in the room.
2. That book was mine
3. There are no apples.
4. Who is in the pool?
5. The bicycle is here.
6. I didn't have a newspaper today.

Chapter 14
- Prepositions

It is useful at this stage to be able to use the prepositions which tell you where something or somebody is, such as in, on, under, over etc. The following list gives most of the usual expressions:

.... *no ue ni*	above, on, over
.... *no shita ni*	under
.... *no mae ni*	in front of
.... *no kochira (-gawa) ni*	on this (side) of
.... *no yoko ni*	beside
.... *no tonari ni*	next to
.... *no migi (-gawa) ni*	to the right of/on the right (side) of
.... *no hidari (-gawa) ni*	to the left of/on the left (side) of
.... *no naka ni*	in/inside
.... *no soto ni*	outside
.... *no ushiro ni*	behind
.... *no mukō (-gawa) ni*	on the other (side) of

Practice 14

Refer to the picture and answer the questions (in Japanese!):

1. Where is the cat?
2. *Ie no mae ni nani ga arimasuka.*
3. Where is the bird?
4. *Sakana wa doko ni imasuka.*
5. Where is the car?

Chapter 15
- Family

Family members		
	Your own	**Other people's**
parents	*ryōshin*	*go-ryōshin*
family	*kazoku*	*go-kazoku*
baby	*aka chan bo* (often just *aka chan*)	
older brother	*ani*	*o-nī san*
older sister	*ane*	*o-nē san*
younger brother	*otōto*	*otōto san*
younger sister	*imōto*	*imōto san*
mother	*haha*	*o-kā san*
father	*chichi*	*o-tō san*
wife	*kanai*	*oku san*
uncle	*oji*	*oji san*
aunt	*oba*	*oba san*
cousin	*itoko*	*o-itoko san*
grandmother	*soba*	*o-bā san*
grandfather	*sofu*	*o-jī san*
grandchild	*mago*	*o-mago san*
husband	*shujin*	*go-shujin*
child	*kodomo*	*kodomo san, o-ko san*
son	*musuko*	*musuko san, botchan*
daughter	*musume*	*musume san, o-jō san*

Notes:

1. There will always be a more polite form for other people's relations
   The *o* and *go* prefixes are honorifics. Generally *o* will come before a word of Japanese origin and *go* before a word of Chinese origin.

2. Husband and wife: the *shu* of *shujin* means "master" or "principal".
   The *jin* is "person". *Kanai* means "inside the house" ('er indoors!).
   Make of that what you will…

3. Notice the difference in pronunciation between grandparents and aunt and uncle.

4. Notice also that there are different words for an older or younger sibling.

5. *Tsuma* - wife, and *otto* - husband can often be used for "the wife/the husband" or the rôle of a wife or a husband.

Chapter 16
- Giving and receiving

As mentioned on page 7, there are two verbs in normal parlance for giving and one for receiving. There are honorific forms of these verbs for when you are giving to or receiving from a superior being but for the moment we are dealing with everyday events.

Giving

If I give to someone else, the verb is *ageru*. If my friend gives to another person, the verb is still *ageru*. BUT if someone else gives to me the verb is *kureru*. This last has the implication that someone is doing you a favour.

Examples

Watashi wa tomodachi ni purezento o agemashita.
I gave my friend a present.

Haruko chan wa Ichiro kun ni purezento o agemashita.
Haruko gave Ichiro a present.

Haruko chan wa watashi ni purezento o kuremashita.
Haruko gave me a present.

But actually, you don't need "*watashi ni*" because if the verb is *kureru*, it must be the speaker who is being given the present, so you could just say *Haruko chan wa purezento o kuremashita*.

Receiving

This is easier. The verb is *morau* and can be used in all polite circumstances.

Examples

Watashi wa tomodachi ni/kara purezento o moraimashita.
I received a present from my friend.

Note that "*ni*" is fine in this context but that you can also use "*kara*" which means "from".

Ichiro kun wa Haruko chan ni/kara purezento o moraimashita.
Ichiro received a present from Haruko.

Chapter 17
- More particles

In the previous chapter we saw the use of *kara*, meaning "from". If you want to express "from Monday to Wednesday" for instance, you can say *getsuyōbi kara suiyōbi made*, *made* meaning "until". You can also use *ni* for "until", so *roku ji kara hachi ji ni*, "from 6 to 8 o'clock".

Just to confuse, you can use *made* and *ni* together to mean "by".

Example: [Bring it] by 6 o'clock. *roku ji made ni [motte kite kudasai.]*

Made can also be used as "to": I am going to Tokyo tomorrow. *Ashita Tōkyo made ikimasu.*

Practice 17

Translate the following:

1. On Sunday I swam from 6.00 to 7.00.

2. Mr. Suzuki will wait for the bus until 9.30.

3. I go to school from Monday to Friday. I don't go on Saturday.

4. I will come back by 3.00 tomorrow.

5. *Nikkō ni kayōbi kara mokuyōbi made imasu.*

6. *Kaigi wa go ji kara desu.*

7. *Furansu jin wa suiyōbi made ni koko ni kimasu.*

8. *Nan de Tokyo kara Yokohama made ikimashitaka.*

Also

The Japanese for "also" is *mo*. Example:
*Kinō banana o kaimashita. Ringo **mo** kaimashita.*
Yesterday I bought some bananas. I **also** bought some apples.

If you are using *mo*, you don't need another particle.

Second example:

Tōkyo ni ikimasu. I am going to Tokyo.

Yokohama ni mo ikimasuka. Are you also going to Yokohama?

The answer could be:

Hai, Yokohama ni mo ikimasu. Yes, I am going to Yokohama too.

or

Iie, Yokohama ni wa/mo ikimasen. No I am not going to Yokohama as well.

Nobody and nothing

Another use for *mo*, after a question word and with a negative verb, is to indicate a negative subject.

Examples: *Dare mo kimasen deshita.* Nobody came.

Hako ni nani ga arimasuka. What is in the box?
Nani mo arimasen. There is nothing.

Tanaka san wa doko desuka. Where is Mr. Tanaka?
Doko ni mo imasen. He isn't anywhere. (Notice the use of *ni* here.)

Chapter 18

- And

This is using "and" between nouns, not with verbs which is a different section altogether.

There are two words for "and" in Japanese: *to* and *ya*.

There is an important difference between them. *To* is used for an exhaustive list of objects whereas *ya* is inexhaustive, but the items mentioned must all belong to the same category.

Examples: On the table there is a book and a pen.
*Tēburu no ue ni hon **to** pen ga arimasu.*

On the table there are books, newspapers, magazines and so on.
*Tēburu no ue ni hon **ya** shinbun **ya** zasshi ga arimasu.*

Practice 18

1. In the garden there are trees and flowers and so on.

2. There are three pens and two pencils on the shelf.

Read this paragraph and then answer the questions:

Yamada san wa doyōbi ni sūpa ni ikimashita. Suzuki san mo ikimashita. Yamada san wa shinbun to zasshii to banana o kaimashita. Suzuki san wa nani mo kaimasen deshita. O-kane ga arimasen deshita. Yamada san wa jū ichi ji made ni kaerimashita.

(a) Where did Mr. Yamada and Mr. Suzuki go? When?

(b) What did Mr. Suzuki buy? Why?

(c) Was Mr. Yamada home by mid-day?

Chapter 19
- Taking leave

In Chapter 3 we dealt with greetings and introductions. This seems a suitable moment to talk about taking one's leave.

The Japanese word many people are familiar with is *sayōnara/sayonara* meaning "goodbye".

I was once told by a Japanese that *sayōnara* is only used if someone is going on a long journey or at the time of a divorce, but I think this is possibly a slight exaggeration!

Other phrases which can be used:

Shitsurei shimasu…	Literally, "I am going to do something rude" but actually more like "Excuse me".
Chotto kaerimasu	*Chotto* means a little or just a minute but is used to soften a statement. *Kaeru* is, of course, to return (possibly home in this case).
Dewa mata ato de	Well, see you later. It can be just *Ja mata*.
Mata ashita	Literally, "again tomorrow" but used as "see you again tomorrow".

You can also say *soro soro* by itself or *soro soro sumimasen ga …* *Soro soro* indicates that it is now time (for you to go). *Sumimasen* is, like *shitsurei shimasu*, an apology, with *ga* ("but" in this case) again softening the statement.

Afterword

There is a huge amount more that can be explained about Japanese grammar, but we don't want to get too complicated at this stage. If you have found this book helpful, please let me know and I shall write another one!

Best wishes for your future study of Japanese.

Rosemary Healing

Ritsuren Koen, Shikoku

Nara

 # Random revision exercises

Can you translate these sentences without looking up?

1. *Endo san wa bengoshi dewa arimasen. Sensei desu.*

2. This is my friend. [She] is Mary.

3. What is your phone number?
   It's 02-579-4381.

4. I'm leaving now. I'll see you tomorrow.

5. *Kono kēki o tabemasenka.*
   Hai, arigatō.

6. *Ano akai kutsu shita o ni soku kudasai.*

7. *Furansu jin desuka.*
   Iie, Itaria jin desu.

8. *Sore wa Tanaka san no zasshi dewa arimasen. Watashi no desu.*

9. Who came yesterday?   Who will come tomorrow?

10. Today is the 1st of April. The day after tomorrow will be Thursday.

11. What is under the table?
    There are two cats.

12. *Nan ji ni kaerimasuka.*

13. *Uchi no mae ni ki ga ni hon arimashita.*

14. *Otōto to imōto wa gakkō ni ikimashita.*

15. *Shujin wa Doitsu jin desu.*

16. Who gave you that present?

17. The meeting lasted from 5.00 to 7.00.

18. *Banana mo ringo mo tabemashita.*

19. My son and daughter will be here on Tuesday.

20. There are cars and bicycles and so on outside the house.

ANSWERS

Chapter 1

Practice 1 (a)

is and is not

1. *Pen dewa arimasen.*
2. *Futobōru desu.*
3. *Orenji dewa arimasen.*
4. *Hottodoggu desu.*
5. *Banana de wa arimasen.*

Practice 1 (b)

was and was not

1. *Tokei dewa arimasen.*
2. *Yūrei desu.*
3. *Basu deshita.*
4. *Iie, Tanaka san dewa arimasen deshita, Yamada san deshita.*

Practice 2

    Boat
    Turkey
    Elevator
    Sausage
    Ball
    Record
    Clarinet
    Knife
    Stewardess
    Interview

Word matching

    Cake
    Coffee
    Computer
    Sandwich
    Baseball
    Television
    Party
    Radio
    Bus
    Chocolate
    Wine
    Ice cream
    Supermarket

NB You can appreciate that *sūpā* is short for "supermarket".
In the same way *ēyakon* is short for "air conditioning" and *terebi* short for "television".

Practice 3

Kon ban wa.

Kon ban wa.

Kochira wa Shimizu san desu.

Takahashi desu. Dōzo yoroshiku.

Yoroshiku o-negaishimasu.

Practice 4

Brazilian, Scottish, Welsh, Spanish, Russian, Dutch

Kochira wa Sumisu san desu. Sumisu san wa Amerika jin desu.

Hajimemashite. Dupont desu.

Dupont san wa Furansu jin desu.

Hajimemashite. Sumisu desu. Dōzo yoroshiku.

Yoroshiku o-negaishimasu.

The above is not cast in stone but is one way of dealing with it.

Chapter 5

This is [Mr.] Roberts. [He] is an English[man] from City Insurance.

Practice 5

Suzuki: *Tanaka san, kon nichi wa.*
Tanaka: *Kon nichi wa. Kochira wa Airando no Fisher san desu.*
Fisher: *Hajimemashite. Dōzo yoroshiku.*
Suzuki: *Yoroshiku o-negaishimasu.*

Hiroshi: *Watashi no pen desu.*
Sachiko: *Iie, watashi no pen desu.*
Teacher: *O-hayō gozaimasu. Watashi no desu. Arigatō.*

Practice 6 (a)

jū san   go jū shi   roku jū hachi   jū ni

Suzuki san no denwa bangō wa zero san no yon nana kyū hachi no roku go ni ichi desu.

Practice 6 (b)

Tokei wa san man go sen nana hayaku en desu.

Kuruma wa happyaku ni jū man en desu.

Hon wa roppyaku kyū jū go en desu.

Numbers:

San zen go hyaku roku jū

Ichi man hassen roppyaku hachi jū go

Yon jū ni man nana hyaku kyū jū kyū

Practice 6 (c)

Kutsu shita o gosoku kudasai.

Hon o sansatsu kudasai.

Kōhī o ippai kudasai.

T-shātsu o nimai kudasai.

Neko o yonhiki kudasai.

Practice 7

1. *Kore wa ¥98 desu.*

2. *Iie, sono tokei wa Amerika no desu.*

   Where is the restaurant?

   Which one?

   That Chinese restaurant.

   Ah! That's over there.

Practice 8

a) *Kore wa hon desu.*

b) *Are wa kuruma de wa arimasen.*

c) *Kamera wa doko desu ka. Koko desu.*

d) *Dore deshita ka.*

e) Is that a flower (over) there?

f) Which house is it?

g) Where is the island? It's over there.

h) This dog is not mine.

Chapter 9

The cat saw the dog.

Practice 9

1. *Kore **wa** watashi **no** kuruma desu.*

2. *Dare **ga** kimasuka.*

3. *Jitensha **de** kimashitaka.*

4. *Sore **wa** Tanaka san **no** tokei desu.*

5. *Sono kamera **o** misete kudasai.*

Practice 10

3.30 on Wednesday, 17th March 2015.

1. *Kyō wa jū ichi gatsu jū yokka desu.*

2. *Ashita wa hachi gatsu tsuitachi desu.*

3. *Kinō wa go gatsu hatsuka deshita.*

4. *Asatte wa jū ni gatsu ni jū shichi nichi doyōbi desu.*

5. *Ototoi wa mokuyōbi deshita.*

   Watashi no tanjōbi wa …[date]…………desu.

Chapter 11

Verb declension

Meaning	Dictionary form	Non-past		Past	
		Positive	Negative	Positive	Negative
GROUP I					
to turn off	kes-u	kesh-imasu	kesh-imasen	kesh-imashita	kesh-imasen deshita
to read	yom-u	yom-imasu	yom-imasen	yom-imashita	yom-imasen deshita
to swim	oyog-u	oyog-imasu	oyog-imasen	oyog-imashita	oyog-imasen deshita
to accept	itadak-u	itadak-imasu	itadak-imasen	itadak-imashita	itadak-imasen deshita
to have/hold	mots-u	moch-imasu	moch-imasen	moch-imashita	moch-imasen deshita
to be wrong	chiga-u	chiga-imasu	chiga-imasen	chiga-imashita	chiga-imasen deshita
to do one's best	gambar-u	gambar-imasu	gambar-imasen	gambar-imashita	gambar-imasen deshita
to last	oyob-u	oyob-imasu	oyob-imasen	oyob-imashita	oyob-imasen deshita
GROUP II					
to give	age-ru	age-masu	age-masen	age-mashita	age-masen deshita
to show	mise-ru	mise-masu	mise-masen	mise-mashita	mise-masen deshita
to shut	shime-ru	shime-masu	shime-masen	shime-mashita	shime-masen deshita
to get off	ori-ru	ori-masu	ori-masen	ori-mashita	ori-masen deshita
to be able	deki-ru	deki-masu	deki-masen	deki-mashita	deki-masen deshita
to begin	hajime-ru	hajime-masu	hajime-masen	hajime-mashita	hajime-masen deshita
to know	shi-ru	shiri-masu	shiri-masen	shiri-mashita	shiri-masen deshita
to advance	susume-ru	susume-masu	susume-masen	susume-mashita	susume-masen deshita

Practice 11

1. *Yamada san ni kakimasu.*
2. *Watashi no inu wa kyō pūru de oyogimashita.*
3. *Basu o machimashita ga, kimasen deshita.*
4. *Suzuki san wa Yokohama ni jū yokka ni ikimashita.*
5. *Sake o nomimasuka.*

1. What is "*shiru*" in English?
2. Won't you open the door?
3. I showed my American camera to Mr. Endo.
4. Mr. Suzuki did not eat any cake yesterday.
5. Hiroshi spoke in Japanese. I didn't understand.

Practice 12 (a)

Meaning	Dictionary form	Non-past		Past	
		Positive	Negative	Positive	Negative
to go	*iku*	*ikimasu*	*ikimasen*	*ikimashita*	*Ikimasen deshita*
to come	*kuru*	*kimasu*	*kimasen*	*kimashita*	*kimasen deshita*
to return	*kaeru*	*kaerimasu*	*kaerimasen*	*kaerimashita*	*kaerimasen deshita*

Practice 12 (b)

1. *Ashita ikimasu.*
2. *Tanaka san wa kinō kimashita.*
3. *Yamada san wa Tōkyō ni kaerimasu.*
4. *Nihon ni kyonen ikimashita.* or *Kyonen Nihon ni ikimashita.*
5. *Kinō kaerimashita.*
6. *Tanaka san wa taishikan ni ikimasen deshita.*
7. *Rai nen kaerimasen.*
8. *Sen shū kimasen deshita.*
9. *Furansu kara kaerimasen deshita.*
10. *Suzuki san wa Doitsu ni kyō ikimasen.*
    (or more or less any other word order as long as the verb comes at the end)
11. *Ashita kimasuka.*
12. *Doko ni ikimasuka. Kaigi ni ikimasu.*

Practice 13

1. *Tanaka san ga daidokoro ni imasu.*
2. *Neko ga niwa ni imasu.*
3. *Shokudō ni e ga arimasu.*
4. *Yamada san no uchi wa Tokyo ni arimasu.*
5. *Kore wa nan desuka.*
6. *Ano hon wa akai desu.*

Translation:

1. *Tanaka san wa heya ni imasen deshita.*
2. *Ano hon wa watashi no deshita.*
3. *Ringo ga arimasen.*
4. *Dare ga pūru ni imasuka.*
5. *Jitensha wa koko [ni arimasu]* (*Desu* could be used here if the sense of the verb is understood).
6. *Kyō shinbun ga arimasen deshita.*

Practice 14

1. *Neko wa ki no shita ni imasu.*
2. *Ie no mae ni hana ga arimasu.*
3. *Tori wa ie no ue ni imasu.*
4. *Sakana wa kawa no naka ni imasu.*
5. *Kuruma wa ie no ushiro ni arimasu.*

Practice 17

1. *Nichiyōbi ni roku ji kara shichi ji made oyogimashita.*
2. *Suzuki san wa ku ji han made basu o machimasu.*
3. *Getsuyōbi kara kinyōbi made gakkō ni ikimasu. Doyōbi ni ikimasen.*
4. *Ashita san ji made ni kaerimasu.*
5. I shall be in Nikkō from Tuesday to Thursday.
6. The meeting is from 5.00.
7. The French people will come here by Wednesday.
8. How [by what means] did you go from Tokyo to Yokohama?

Practice 18

1. *Niwa ni ki ya hana ga arimasu.*
2. *Tana ni pen ga san bon to enpitsu ga ni hon arimasu.*

Mr. Yamada went to the supermarket on Tuesday. Mr. Suzuki went too. Mr. Yamada bought a newspaper, a magazine and bananas. Mr. Suzuki didn't buy anything. He had no money.
Mr. Yamada got home by 11.00

Random revision exercises

1. Mr. Endo is not a lawyer. He's a teacher.
2. *Kochira wa watashi no tomodachi desu. Mērī desu.*
3. *O-denwa bangō wa nanban desu ka.*
   (The honorific *o* is attached for politeness.)
   Zero ni no go nana kyū no yon san hachi ichi desu.

4. *Chotto kaerimasu. Mata ashita.*
   (This is just one way of translating this.)

5. Won't you eat this cake?
   Yes, thank you.

6. Two pairs of those red socks over there, please.

7. Are you French?
   No, I'm Italian.

8. That is not Mr. Tanaka's magazine. It's mine.

9. *Kinō dare ga kimashitaka. Ashita dare ga kimasuka.*

10. *Kyō wa shi gatsu tsuitachi desu. Asatte wa mokuyōbi desu.*

11. *Tēburu no shita ni nani ga arimasuka.*
    Neko ga ni hiki imasu.

12. What time will you come back?

13. There were two trees in front of the house.

14. My (younger) brother and sister went to school.

15. My husband is German.

16. *Dare ga ano purezento o agemashitaka.*

17. *Kaigi wa go ji kara shichi ji made oyobimashita.*

18. I ate a banana as well as an apple.

19. *Musuko to musume wa kayōbi ni koko ni imasu.*

20. *Uchi no soto ni kuruma ya jitensha ga arimasu.*

Utsukushima

Glossary - Japanese/English

A	
achira	that over there/over there
ageru	to give
akachan	baby
akai	red
akeru	to open
aki	Autumn
Amerika	America
ane, o-nēsan	sister (older)
ani, o-nīsan	brother (older)
ano	that + noun, away from speaker and listener
are	that, away from speaker and listener
arigatō	thank you
aru/iru	to be
aru/motsu	to have/to hold
asatte	day after tomorrow
ashita/asu	tomorrow
asoko	over there
asu/ashita	tomorrow
ato	afterwards, later
B	
bangō	number
bengoshi	lawyer
C	
chan	suffix after a name: children, girls
chichi, o-tōsan	father
chigau	to be wrong
chō	trillion
chotto	a little
Chūgoku	China
D	
dai	counter for machines

daidokoro	kitchen
dare	who?
de	particle: by means of, at
dekiru	to be able
densha	train (electric vehicle)
denwa	telephone
desu	is, are
dewa...	well...
do yōbi	Saturday
dochira	which?, of two things
dōitashimashite	don't mention it
Doitsu	Germany
doko	where?
dōmo	quite, very: used as "thanks"
donata	who? (more formal than *dare*)
dono	which? + noun
dore	which?, of more than two things
dōzo	please
dōzo yoroshiku	I'm pleased to meet you.
E	
e	particle: direction towards, to
e	picture
Eikoku	England/UK
enpitsu	pencil
F	
Furansu	France
futatsu	two
futsuka	date: 2nd
fuyu	Winter
G	
ga	but, in the middle of a sentence
ga	particle: subject marker after some question words, and in random statements
gai rai go	borrowed words language coming from overseas

gakkō	school
gakusei	student
ganbaru	to do one's best
gatsu	month
getsu yōbi	Monday
go	five
go	language
go gatsu	May
go-shujin, shujin, otto	husband
gozaimasu	polite form of *desu*
H	
hachi	eight
hachi gatsu	August
haha, o-kāsan	mother
hai	counter for glass/cupfuls
hai	yes (you are right)
hajimemashite	how do you do?
hajimeru	to begin
hako	box
han	half
hana	flower
hanasu	to speak
haru	Spring
hatsuka	date: 20th
heya	room
hidari	left (on the left)
hiki	counter for small animals
hitotsu	one
hon	book
hon	counter for cylindrical objects
hyaku	hundred
I	
ichi	one
ichi gatsu	January

Igirisu	England/UK
ie	house
iie	no
iku	to go
ikura	how much?
ikutsu	how many?
imōto, imōtosan	sister (younger)
inu	dog
iru/aru	to be
isogu	to hurry
itadaku	to accept
Itaria	Italy
itoko, o-itokosan	cousin
itsu	when?
itsuka	date: 5th
itsutsu	five
J	
ji	time, o'clock
jin	person
jitensha	bicycle (self-turning vehicle)
jū gatsu	October
jū ichi gatsu	November
jū ni gatsu	December
jū/jyū	ten
K	
ka	question marker
ka yōbi	Tuesday
kaeru	to return
kaigi	meeting
kaku	to write
kanai, okusan, tsuma	wife
kara	particle: from
kau	to buy
kawa	river

kazoku	family
kēki	cake
kesu	to turn off
ki	tree
kin yōbi	Friday
kinō	yesterday
kochira	this (person or place)
kodomo, kodomosan, o-kosan	child
kōhi	coffee
koko	here
kokonoka	date: 9th
kokonotsu	nine
kon ban wa	good evening
kon nichi wa	hello, good day
kono	this + noun, near speaker
kore	this, near speaker
ku gatsu	September
ku/kyū	nine
kudasai	please
kudasaru	to give (from superior to speaker)
kun	suffix after a name: boys
kureru	to give (to me)
kuru	to come
kuruma	car
kutsu shita	sock(s)
kyō	today
M	
made	particle: until, to
made ni	particle: by
mae	in front of
mago, o-magosan	grandchild
mai	counter for flat, thin things
man	ten thousand
mata	again

matsu	to wait
migi	right (on the right)
mikka	date: 3rd
miru	to see
mise	shop
miseru	to show
mittsu	three
mo	particle: also
moku yōbi	Thursday
morau	to receive
motsu/aru	to have/to hold
muika	date: 6th
mukō	other side (of)
musuko, musukosan, botchan	son
musume, musumesan, o-jōsan	daughter
muttsu	six
N	
naka	inside
nan/nani	what?
nanatsu	seven
nanoka	date: 7th
natsu	Summer
neko	cat
nen	year
ni	in
ni	particle: direction towards, on, in, to
ni	two
ni gatsu	February
nichi yōbi	Sunday
Nihon	Japan
niwa	garden
no	particle: possession
nomu	to drink

O	
oba, obasan	aunt
o-hayō gozaimasu	good morning
o-itokosan, itoko	cousin
oji, ojisan	uncle
o-kane	money
o-kāsan, haha	mother
oku	billion
okusan, kanai, tsuma	wife
o-magosan, mago	grandchild
o-negai shimasu	please
o-nēsan, ane	sister (older)
o-nīsan, ani	brother (older)
oriru	to get off
o-tōsan, chichi	father
otōto, otōtosan	brother (younger)
ototoi	day before yesterday
otto, go-shujin, shujin	husband
o-yasumi nasai	good night
oyobu	to last
oyogu	to swim
P	
pūru	pool
R	
ringo	apple
roku	six
roku gatsu	June
ryōshin	parents
S	
sakana	fish
sakura	cherry blossom
sama	suffix after a name: superior
san	suffix after a name: Mr., Mrs., Miss
san	three
san gatsu	March

sashiageru	give (to superior)
satsu	counter for books
sayōnara/sayonara	goodbye
sen	a line
sen	thousand
sensei	teacher
shi	four
shi gatsu	April
shichi	seven
shichi gatsu	July
shima	island
shimeru	to shut
shinbun	newspaper
shinu	to die
shiru	to know
shita	under
shitsurei shimasu	excuse me
shokudō	dining room
shū	week
shujin, go-shujin, otto	husband
soba, o-bāsan	grandmother
sochira	that/there
sofu, o-jīsan	grandfather
soko	there
soku	counter for pairs
sono	that + noun, near listener
sore	that, near listener
soro soro	now (it's time)
soto	outside
sui yōbi	Wednesday
sumimasen	excuse me
suru	to do
susumeru	to advance
T	
taberu	to eat
taishikan	embassy

tana	shelf
tanjōbi	birthday
to, ya	and
tō	ten
tōka	date: 10th
tokei	watch
tomodachi	friend
tonari	next to
tori	bird
toshi	year (alternative reading)
tsuitachi	date: 1st
tsukau	to use
tsuma, okusan, kanai	wife
U	
uchi	house
ue	above, over
ushiro	behind
W	
wa	particle: topic marker
wakaru	to understand
watashi	I (personal pronoun)
Y	
yattsu	eight
yen/en	Japanese national currency
yobu	to call
yottsu	four
yōka	date: 8th
yokka	date: 4th
yoko	beside
yomu	to read
yon	four
yoroshiku onegaishimasu	I'm pleased to meet you too.
yūrei	ghost
Z	
zasshi	magazine

Glossary - English/Japanese

A	
above, over	ue
afterwards, later	ato
again	mata
a line	sen
a little	chotto
also	mo
America	Amerika
and	to, ya
apple	ringo
April	shi gatsu
August	hachi gatsu
aunt	oba, obasan
Autumn	aki
B	
baby	akachan
behind	ushiro
beside	yoko
bicycle (self-turning vehicle)	jitensha
billion	oku
bird	tori
birthday	tanjōbi
book	hon
borrowed words	gai rai go
box	hako
brother (older)	ani, o-nīsan
brother (younger)	otōto, otōtosan
but, in the middle of a sentence	ga
by	made ni

C	
cake	kēki
car	kuruma
cat	neko
cherry blossom	sakura
child	kodomo, kodomosan, o-kosan
China	Chūgoku
coffee	kōhi
counter for books	satsu
counter for cylindrical objects	hon
counter for flat, thin things	mai
counter for glass/cupfuls	hai
counter for machines	dai
counter for pairs	soku
counter for small animals	hiki
cousin	itoko, o-itokosan
D	
date: 1st	tsuitachi
date: 2nd	futsuka
date: 3rd	mikka
date: 4th	yokka
date: 5th	itsuka
date: 6th	muika
date: 7th	nanoka
date: 8th	yōka
date: 9th	kokonoka
date: 10th	tōka
date: 20th	hatsuka
daughter	musume, musumesan, o-jōsan
day after tomorrow	asatte
day before yesterday	ototoi

December	jū ni gatsu
dining room	shokudō
dog	inu
don't mention it	dōitashimashite
door	dōa
E	
eight	hachi, yattsu
embassy	taishikan
England/UK	Eikoku/Igirisu
excuse me	shitsurei shimasu/sumimasen
F	
family	kazoku
father	chichi, o-tōsan
February	ni gatsu
fish	sakana
five	go, itsutsu
flower	hana
four	shi, yottsu
France	Furansu
Friday	kin yōbi
friend	tomodachi
from	kara
G	
garden	niwa
Germany	Doitsu
ghost	yūrei
give (from superior to speaker)	kudasaru
give (polite)	ageru
give (to me)	kureru
give (to superior)	sashiageru
goodbye	sayōnara/sayonara

good evening	kon ban wa
good morning	o-hayō gozaimasu
good night	o-yasumi nasai
grandchild	mago, o-magosan
grandfather	sofu, o-jīsan
grandmother	soba, o-bāsan

H

half	han
hello, good day	kon nichi wa
here	koko
house	uchi/ie
how do you do?	hajimemashite
how many?	ikutsu
how much?	ikura
hundred	hyaku
husband	shujin, go-shujin, otto

I

I (personal pronoun)	watashi
I'm pleased to meet you.	dōzo yoroshiku
I'm pleased to meet you too.	yoroshiku onegaishimasu
in	ni
in front of	mae
inside	naka
is, are	desu
island	shima
Italy	Itaria

J

January	ichi gatsu
Japan	Nihon
Japanese national currency	yen/en

July	shichi gatsu
June	roku gatsu
K	
kitchen	daidokoro
L	
language	go
language coming from overseas	gai rai go
last year	kyo nen
lawyer	bengoshi
left (on the left)	hidari
M	
magazine	zasshi
March	san gatsu
May	go gatsu
meeting	kaigi
Monday	getsu yōbi
money	o-kane
month	gatsu
mother	haha, o-kāsan
N	
newspaper	shinbun
next to	tonari
next year	rai nen
nine	ku/kyū, kokonotsu
no	iie
November	jū ichi gatsu
now (it's time)	soro soro
number	bangō
O	
October	jū gatsu
one	ichi, hitotsu
other side of	mukō
outside	soto
over there	asoko

P	
parents	ryōshin
particle: also	mo
particle: by	made ni
particle: by means of, at	de
particle: direction towards, on, in, to	ni
particle: direction towards, to	e
particle: from	kara
particle: object marker	o
particle: possession	no
particle: question marker	ka
particle: subject marker after some question words, and in random statements	ga
particle: topic marker	wa
particle: until, to	made
pencil	enpitsu
person	jin
picture	e
please	dōzo
please	kudasai
please	o-negai shimasu
polite form of *desu*	gozaimasu
pool	pūru
Q	
question marker	ka
quite, very: used as "thanks"	dōmo
R	
red	akai
right (on the right)	migi
river	kawa
room	heya
S	
Saturday	do yōbi
school	gakkō
September	ku gatsu

seven	shichi, nanatsu
shelf	tana
shop	mise
sister (older)	ane, o-nē san
sister (younger)	imōto, imōto san
six	roku, muttsu
sock(s)	kutsu shita
son	musuko, musukosan, botchan
Spring	haru
student	gakusei
suffix after a name of a person senior to the speaker	sama
suffix after a name: boys	kun
suffix after a name: children, girls	chan
suffix after a name: Mr., Mrs., Miss	san
Summer	natsu
Sunday	nichi yōbi
T	
teacher	sensei
telephone	denwa
ten	jū/jyū, tō
ten thousand	man
thanks	dōmo
thank you	arigatō
that , away from speaker and listener	are
that + noun, away from speaker and listener	ano
that + noun, near listener	sono
that over there/over there	achira
that, near listener	sore
that/there	sochira
there	soko
this (person or place)	kochira
this + noun, near speaker	kono
this, near speaker	kore

this year	kotoshi
thousand	sen
three	san, mittsu
Thursday	moku yōbi
time, o'clock	ji
to accept	itadaku
to advance	susumeru
to be	aru/iru
to be able	dekiru
to be wrong	chigau
to begin	hajimeru
to buy	kau
to call	yobu
to come	kuru
to die	shinu
to do	suru
to do one's best	ganbaru
to drink	nomu
to eat	taberu
to get off	oriru
to give	ageru/sashiageru/kureru/kudasaru
to go	iku
to have/to hold	aru/motsu
to hurry	isogu
to know	shiru
to last	oyobu
to open	akeru
to read	yomu
to receive	morau
to return	kaeru
to see	miru
to show	miseru

to shut	shimeru
to speak	hanasu
to swim	oyogu
to turn off	kesu
to understand	wakaru
to use	tsukau
to wait	matsu
to write	kaku
today	kyō
tomorrow	ashita/asu
train	densha
tree	ki
trillion	chō
Tuesday	ka yōbi
two	ni, futatsu
U	
uncle	oji, ojisan
under	shita
until	made
W	
watch	tokei
Wednesday	sui yōbi
week	shū
well...	dewa...
what?	nan/nani
when?	itsu
where?	doko
which? + noun	dono
which?, of more than two things	dore
which?, of two things	dochira
who?	dare
who? (more formal than *dare*)	donata
wife	kanai, okusan, tsuma
Winter	fuyu

Y	
year	nen/toshi (alternative reading)
yes (you are right)	hai
yesterday	kinō

Writing Practice Charts

Please feel free to copy these charts for your own use

Hiragana

あ a	い i	う u	え e	お o
か ka	き ki	く ku	け ke	こ ko
さ sa	し shi	す su	せ se	そ so
た ta	ち chi	つ tsu	て te	と to
な na	に ni	ぬ nu	ね ne	の no
は ha	ひ hi	ふ fu	へ he	ほ ho
ま ma	み mi	む mu	め me	も mo
や ya		ゆ yu		よ yo
ら ra	り ri	る ru	れ re	ろ ro
わ wa				を w/o
ん n				

Katakana

ア a	イ i	ウ u	エ e	オ o
カ ka	キ ki	ク ku	ケ ke	コ ko
サ sa	シ shi	ス su	セ se	ソ so
タ ta	チ chi	ツ tsu	テ te	ト to
ナ na	ニ ni	ヌ nu	ネ ne	ノ no
ハ ha	ヒ hi	フ fu	ヘ he	ホ ho
マ ma	ミ mi	ム mu	メ me	モ mo
ヤ ya		ユ yu		ヨ yo
ラ ra	リ ri	ル ru	レ re	ロ ro
ワ wa				ヲ w/o
ン n				

Hiragana

a	i	u	e	o
ka	ki	ku	ke	ko
sa	shi	su	se	so
ta	chi	tsu	te	to
na	ni	nu	ne	no
ha	hi	fu	he	ho
ma	mi	mu	me	mo
ya		yu		yo
ra	ri	ru	re	ro
wa				(w)o
				n

Katakana

a	i	u	e	o
ka	ki	ku	ke	ko
sa	shi	su	se	so
ta	chi	tsu	te	to
na	ni	nu	ne	no
ha	hi	fu	he	ho
ma	mi	mu	me	mo
ya		yu		yo
ra	ri	ru	re	ro
wa				(w)o
				n

Practice Chart 1

a	i	u	e	o
ka	ki	ku	ke	ko
sa	shi	su	se	so
ta	chi	tsu	te	to
na	ni	nu	ne	no
ha	hi	fu	he	ho
ma	mi	mu	me	mo
ya		yu		yo
ra	ri	ru	re	ro
wa				(w)o
				n

Practice Chart 2

Practice Chart 2

Byodoin Temple, Uji

Book designed by

www.ingramcontent.com/pod-product-compliance
Lightning Source LLC
Chambersburg PA
CBHW040508240426
43662CB00050B/2466